HOW TO
HELP STUDENTS COMPLETE CLASSWORK AND HOMEWORK ASSIGNMENTS

Timothy E. Heron
Brooke J. Hippler
Matthew J. Tincani

HOW TO IMPROVE CLASSROOM BEHAVIOR SERIES

SERIES EDITORS

Saul Axelrod
Steven C. Mathews

pro·ed
An International Publisher

8700 Shoal Creek Boulevard
Austin, Texas 78757-6897
800/897-3202   Fax 800/397-7633
www.proedinc.com

© 2003 by PRO-ED, Inc.
8700 Shoal Creek Boulevard
Austin, Texas 78757-6897
800/897-3202   Fax 800/397-7633
www.proedinc.com

All rights reserved. No part of the material protected by this copyright notice may be reproduced or used in any form or by any means, electronic or mechanical, including photocopying, recording, or by any information storage and retrieval system, without prior written permission of the copyright owner.

Library of Congress Cataloging-in-Publication Data

Heron, Timothy E.
    How to help students complete classwork and homework assignments / Timothy E. Heron, Brooke J. Hippler, Matthew J. Tincani.
        p.   cm. — (How to improve classroom behavior series)
    Includes bibliographical references (p.).
    ISBN 0-89079-913-X
    1. Classroom management.   2. Behavior modification.   3. Homework.   I. Hippler, Brooke J.   II. Tincani, Matthew J.   III. Title.   IV. Series.

LB3013.H47   2003
371.102'4—dc21
                                                                    2002033303

This book is designed in Minion and Gill Sans.

Printed in the United States of America

1   2   3   4   5   6   7   8   9   10   06   05   04   03   02

*To our colleagues and families, notably
John Cooper, Ralph Gardner III, Bill Heward, and
Diane Sainato, Marge, Kathy, and Christine,
Jeff, Brandon, Ashley, and Delaney,
and
Jennifer*

CONTENTS

Foreword ❦ vii

Preface to Series ❦ ix

Acknowledgment ❦ xiii

Introduction   1

Part I: Increasing Classwork Productivity   2

Part II: Increasing Homework Productivity   15

Final Examination ❦ 47

Answer Key ❦ 54

References and Further Readings ❦ 57

About the Authors ❦ 59

FOREWORD

Having spent several years as a classroom teacher, as a principal of both regular and special education students, and as an educational researcher, it has long been apparent to me that there is a need for materials that provide quick solutions to specific classroom problems. The *How To Improve Classroom Behavior Series* edited by Saul Axelrod and Steven C. Mathews fills that need. Although there have been a number of excellent research studies and texts that present effective classroom management techniques, the beauty of this series is that the authors have used their own experiences and surveyed the literature to present effective procedures that efficiently guide teachers toward solutions of common classroom management problems.

The value of such a series should be apparent. Teachers faced with particular problems, such as students who are disruptive or who bully or tease, can consult the series for solutions. Ideally these books will be found on a bookshelf in the teachers' lounge. Without having to search through professional journals or cumbersome texts, teachers will easily be able to focus on the particular behavior that is a topic of concern. Principals, school psychologists, counselors, and other professionals to whom teachers sometimes refer students with problem behaviors, will also find these texts useful in providing solutions for teachers. It also should prove extremely helpful, especially to beginning teachers, when a principal or psychologist can provide a simple, uncluttered text that tells the teacher exactly what to do in certain problem situations.

The booklets in the series are presented in such a way that they help the user to clearly define the behavior of concern and then to implement step-by-step programs that deal effectively with that behavior. Because the booklets are written in straightforward, nontechnical language, teachers will not become bogged down in trying to understand psychological jargon or complex procedures.

Saul Axelrod is a respected researcher and author. He has published more than 60 research articles and book chapters on behavior and eight books that deal with classroom problems. An excellent writer, he has served on the editorial boards of ten prominent psychological and educational journals. As a licensed psychologist and professor of special education, he has wide experience in instructing teachers in the use of classroom management techniques. Due to his extensive experience and many professional contacts, he and his coeditor were able to select authors well qualified to write each booklet in the series.

Steven C. Mathews is an educator who has spent over 30 years in educational publishing, including stints as managing editor of education for the College Division of Allyn & Bacon and as editor in chief of PRO-ED. He served two terms as president of the Austin, Texas, Chapter of the Council for Exceptional Children and has served on advisory committees for the American Speech-Language-Hearing Association, Council for Learning Disabilities, and Texas Council for Exceptional Children. His publications include tests and therapy materials.

It has been my privilege to work closely with both Saul and Steve. I participated with Saul in several of his first research publications and coauthored with him my most recent publication. I know firsthand that he is an excellent researcher, teacher, and author. I know of no one better qualified to produce this series. I have also worked closely with Steve, who served as managing editor for a number of my publications, including my own *How To Manage Behavior Series*. His skill in guiding the selection of topics and in shaping and polishing manuscripts is unparalleled in my experience. Their cooperative efforts make this series a valuable contribution to the field of teacher education.

R. Vance Hall
Professor Emeritus
University of Kansas

PREFACE TO SERIES

The idea for the *How To Improve Classroom Behavior Series* grew from our conversations with R. Vance Hall. His popular series of booklets called *How To Manage Behavior* presents, in a step-by-step manner, behavioral procedures and techniques. Although they are practical and quick to read, the booklets in his series do not easily show a teacher who may be unfamiliar with behavioral techniques which ones would be best to use in specific situations. We agreed that a new series was needed—a series that would present behavioral techniques in booklets that each address a specific problem behavior that teachers encounter in their classrooms.

Development of the Series

We first wanted to determine what common behavior problems occur in the classroom. In reviewing the literature (Bender, 1987; Bibou-Nakou, Kiosseoglou, & Stogiannidou, 2000; Bickerstaff, Leon, & Hudson, 1997; Elam, 1987, 1989; Elam, Rose, & Gallup, 1994; Fagen, 1986; Gibbons & Jones, 1994; Greenlee & Ogletree, 1993; Jones, Quah, & Charlton, 1996; Malone, Bonitz, & Rickett, 1998; Mastrilli & Brown, 1999; Ordover, 1997), we found that common classroom behavior problems were consistently reported regardless of the age of the student, the type of classroom, the special needs of the student, the experience of the teacher, the passage of time, or the part of the world. This review produced a preliminary list of possible topics for the series.

The preliminary list was then compared to topics presented in textbooks used in courses on behavior management and classroom discipline (e.g., Charles, 1999; Kaplan, 1995, 2000; Sloane, 1988; Walker & Walker, 1991; Workman & Katz, 1995). The list was also evaluated by educators and psychologists from university and other school settings. Their input helped us create a revised list of topics.

The final list of topics, reflected in the titles of the *How To Improve Classroom Behavior Series*, was created by combining topics that had common themes and eliminating topics that did not lend themselves to the format of the series. After the final list was completed, we contacted potential authors for each booklet. Each author selected has a background related to the topic, knowledge of current behavioral principles, and experience working directly with teachers and students.

Format of the Series

All the booklets in the series were written in the same format. Each booklet includes the following:

- Practical and nontechnical information
- All the information a teacher needs to implement a strategy
- Step-by-step strategy presentation
- Numerous strategy suggestions from which the reader can choose
- Numerous examples of various levels of problem severity, ages of students, and instructional settings
- Interactive learning procedures with space and prompts for the reader to make oral or written responses
- References and suggestions for further readings

Uses of the Series

Each of the booklets in the series may be used independently or in conjunction with the other booklets. Each can be read and the information used by regular classroom teachers, special education teachers, teachers in collaborative classrooms, school psychologists, and anyone else who has students who exhibit the behavior that is the topic of the booklet.

The design of the booklets allows them to be used without additional information. However, they also lend themselves to workshop, in-service, or consultation situations. They are ideal for a special education teacher, school psychologist, or other consultant to share with a teacher who requests information or who reports a problem in her or his classroom.

Acknowledgments

We would first like to thank our friend R. Vance Hall for his advice, counsel, and patience, and for his writing the foreword to the series. The series would not exist without Vance's contributions.

We would also like to thank the contributors to the series. They all have prepared manuscripts following a prescribed format in a very short period of time. The many people at PRO-ED who have contributed to the series from its inception through its publication also have earned our thanks and respect.

Saul Axelrod and
Steven C. Mathews
Series Editors

Series References

Bender, W. N. (1987). Correlates of classroom behavior problems among learning disabled and nondisabled children in mainstream classes. *Learning Disabilities Quarterly, 10,* 317–324.

Bibou-Nakou, I., Kiosseoglou, G., & Stogiannidou, A. (2000). Elementary teacher's perceptions regarding school behavior problems: Implications for school psychological services. *Psychology in the Schools, 37,* 123–134.

Bickerstaff, S., Leon, S. H., & Hudson, J. G. (1997). Preserving the opportunity for education: Texas' alternative education programs for disruptive youth. *Journal of Law and Education, 26,* 1–39.

Charles, C. M. (1999). *Building classroom discipline* (6th ed.). New York: Longman.

Elam, S. M. (1987). Differences between educators and the public on questions of education policy. *Phi Delta Kappan, 69,* 294–296.

Elam, S. M. (1989). The second Gallup/Phi Delta Kappa poll of teachers' attitudes toward the public schools. *Phi Delta Kappan, 70,* 785–798.

Elam, S. M., Rose, L. C., & Gallup, A. M. (1994). The 26th annual Phi Delta Kappa/Gallup poll of the public's attitude toward the public schools. *Phi Delta Kappan, 76,* 41–56.

Fagen, S. A. (1986). Least intensive interventions for classroom behavior problems. *Pointer, 31,* 21–28.

Gibbons, L., & Jones, L. (1994). Novice teachers' reflectivity upon their classroom management. (ERIC Documentation Reproduction Service No. ED386446)

Greenlee, A. R., & Ogletree, E. J. (1993). Teachers' attitude toward student discipline problems and classroom management strategies. (ERIC Documentation Reproduction Service No. ED364330)

Jones, K., Quah, M. L., & Charlton, T. (1996). Behaviour which primary and special school teachers in Singapore find most troublesome. *Research in Education, 55,* 62–73.

Kaplan, J. S. (1995). *Beyond behavior modification: A cognitive–behavioral approach to behavior management in the school* (3rd ed.). Austin, TX: PRO-ED.

Kaplan, J. S. (2000). *Beyond functional assessment: A social–cognitive approach to the evaluation of behavior problems in children and youth.* Austin, TX: PRO-ED.

Malone, B. G., Bonitz, D. A., & Rickett, M. M. (1998). Teacher perceptions of disruptive behavior: Maintaining instructional focus. *Educational Horizons, 76,* 189–194.

Mastrilli, T. M., & Brown, D. S. (1999). Elementary student teachers' cases: An analysis of dilemmas and solutions. *Action in Teacher Education, 21,* 50–60.

Ordover, E. (1997). *Inclusion of students with disabilities who are labled "disruptive": Issues papers for legal advocates and parents.* Boston: Center for Law and Education.

Sloane, H. N. (1988). *The good kid book: How to solve the 16 most common behavior problems.* Champaign, IL: Research Press.

Walker, H. M., & Walker, J. E. (1991). *Coping with noncompliance in the classroom: A positive approach for teachers.* Austin, TX: PRO-ED.

Workman, E. A., & Katz, A. M. (1995). *Teaching behavioral self-control to students* (2nd ed.). Austin, TX: PRO-ED.

How To Improve Classroom Behavior Series

How To Help Students Remain Seated
How To Deal Effectively with Lying, Stealing, and Cheating
How To Prevent and Safely Manage Physical Aggression and Property Destruction
How To Help Students Complete Classwork and Homework Assignments
How To Help Students Play and Work Together
How To Deal with Students Who Challenge and Defy Authority
How To Deal Effectively with Whining and Tantrum Behaviors
How To Help Students Follow Directions, Pay Attention, and Stay on Task

ACKNOWLEDGMENT

The authors thank Mr. Michael Plummer for his artistic contributions to Figures 5 and 10.

Introduction

Teachers assign classwork and homework to provide practice for their students and to help ensure mastery of specific content. Sometimes the classwork or homework is assigned for solo practice, with the expectation that it will be performed independently. At other times, it is assigned within student dyads, groups, or as part of a cooperative project that extends over many weeks or months. In any case, classwork and homework arguably play a central role in students' academic curricula because such work (a) increases opportunities for students to respond, (b) creates occasions for active student responses, and (c) provides teachers with feedback on the quality of instruction (Greenwood, Delquadri, & Hall, 1984; Heward, 1994).

Still another benefit for well-designed classwork and homework relates to generality and maintenance of behavior change. Teachers also provide classwork and homework to determine if behaviors demonstrated during daily instruction are evident in different contexts (i.e., Can the student solve a higher order problem after instruction on a lower level skill? Are skills maintained in the future?).

Also, although not often recognized, homework provides an opportunity for parents to participate in the learning processes of their child. Even if ethnic, cultural, and socioeconomic family practices and dynamics, or language skills mitigate against active participation, parents can still be home-based partners if they supervise their child's work. Regardless of the child's level—elementary, middle, or high school—parents can be extremely influential in helping to reinforce skills introduced by teachers.

The purpose of this book is to address strategies that teachers, parents, and students can use to facilitate the accurate, timely, and proficient completion of classwork and homework assignments. Part I addresses increasing classwork productivity. Part II addresses increasing homework productivity. A range of examples is provided across elementary, middle, and high school levels for students with and without disabilities. Emphasis is placed on practical procedures that meet the standard of best practice (Peters & Heron, 1993).

PART I: Increasing Classwork Productivity

Have you ever had the proverbial "bump-on-a-log" student in your classroom? You know who we mean: the student who, despite your best efforts, does not finish in-class assignments, or if he or she does, turns in work that is incomplete, sloppy, or riddled with errors. These students present real challenges to teachers with respect to assignment completion. If they do not engage in structured in-class assignments, they are more likely to seek attention through less acceptable means (i.e., disruptions). Surely, the stakes for these students increase as they move from elementary to middle to high school levels. Predictably, a pattern of poor classwork, coupled with a rising tide of disruptions, characterizes the profile of many of these students.

So how can a teacher increase classwork productivity for students? Let's begin by quickly stating that punishment (using aversive consequences in an ill-conceived attempt to generate student compliance and productivity) is not the answer. Although many teachers (and parents) use punishment frequently as a method to gain compliance, it does not represent a long-term solution.

Fortunately, teachers have many strategies they can use to increase the quantity and quality of student classwork. A good way to conceptualize the range of available strategies is to consider a matrix of preteaching, teaching, and postteaching options distributed across environmental, instructional/management, and reinforcement/feedback areas (Wood, 2002). Conceptualizing an arrangement of strategies is helpful because it allows the teacher to design, implement, and evaluate procedures across configurations.

Table 1 shows a matrix of preteaching, teaching, and postteaching strategies that have been demonstrated to be effective, to follow best practice procedures, and to be likely to increase student productivity.

TABLE 1
Select Preteaching, Teaching, and Postteaching Strategies Factored Across Environmental, Instructional/Management, and Reinforcement/Feedback Areas

	Preteaching	**Teaching**	**Postteaching**
Environment	Grouping	Seating arrangements	Grading options
Instruction and Management	Mode of presentation; Mode of response	Correcting student errors	
Reinforcement and Feedback	Individual versus group consequences; Schedules of reinforcement	Charting performance	

Note. Adapted from *The Educational Consultant: Helping Professionals, Parents, and Students in Inclusive Classrooms* (4th ed., p. 388), by T. Heron and K. Harris, 2001, Austin, TX: PRO-ED. Copyright 2001 by PRO-ED, Inc. Adapted with permission.

Question 1

How does the matrix shown in Table 1 assist teachers with programming in-class assignments?

_____
_____
_____
_____
_____

Preteaching

Grouping

Students can be grouped in one of three basic configurations: large-group, small-group, and one-to-one arrangements. To increase productivity, teachers who rely exclusively on large-group, lecture-style arrangements might consider changing to small-group configurations. A good way to accomplish this is to institute a formalized tutoring system or a cooperative learning arrangement in the class (Heron & Harris, 2001). In the tutoring arrangement, students work in smaller groups, thereby increasing the number of active response opportunities (practice), positive and corrective feedback events, and reinforcement statements for correct responses to the content. Within a 10- to 15-minute period, student pairs can generate, after training, a large number of practice opportunities, feedback statements, and vocal reinforcers, all of which contribute to the assignment being completed. Figure 1 shows a small group of tutors and tutees who switch roles to teach each other individualized content recorded on index cards. The right panel of the folder holds the instructional materials (cards), and the left panel shows a graph that records student daily performance.

Figure 1. Small dyadic group of tutors and tutees. *Note.* From *The Educational Consultant: Helping Professionals, Parents, and Students in Inclusive Classrooms* (4th ed., p. 453), by T. Heron and K. Harris, 2001, Austin, TX: PRO-ED. Copyright 2001 by PRO-ED, Inc. Reprinted with permission.

Question 2

What is an effect of having students arranged in tutor–tutee dyads with respect to practice and reinforcement?

Similarly, cooperative learning arrangements, defined as small groups of students working in teams to complete a task, are a viable alternative for meeting the individual needs of students, especially those who might have special needs, in inclusive classrooms. Given appropriate directions, incentives, and task structures, students gain interdependence during face-to-face interactions with peers, and the efforts of all members are needed for group accomplishment of the goal (i.e., productivity with the task). As important collateral effects, student leadership, decision making, trust building, and conflict-management skills can be learned.

Question 3

Define cooperative learning and state the main and collateral effects that can be achieved by implementing it.

Mode of Presentation and Mode of Response

Imagine the following dialogue in a middle school classroom.

> TEACHER: "Ming, can you tell me the principal north–south river that bisects the United States?"
>
> MING (sinking lower in her seat while sheepishly replying): "No."
>
> TEACHER (a bit annoyed and impatient): "We mentioned this river yesterday, don't you remember?"
>
> MING (embarrassed): "I can't remember."
>
> TEACHER: "Sara, can you help Ming?" (Teacher moves on.)

In this vignette, it seems clear that the teacher used a question–answer format in a futile attempt to evoke a correct response. Her method of presentation was vocal, and her expected mode of response was vocal. In the absence of a correct response, the teacher moved on to Sara, leaving Ming embarrassed and perhaps less motivated to try again. Now examine a similar dialogue in which the teacher, when receiving the same incorrect response, changes the expected mode of response, thereby permitting student success.

> TEACHER: "Ming, can you tell me the principal north–south river that bisects the United States?"
>
> MING (sinking lower in her seat while sheepishly replying): "No."
>
> TEACHER (heads to the front of the room and pulls down a map): "We mentioned this river yesterday, and it's located in the central United States. Come up to the map with me and let's see if we

can find it. Can you *point* to the river that bisects the midsection of the country?"

MING (approaching the map): "Here it is."

TEACHER (smiling): "That's right. What's its name? Look in the blue section."

MING (beaming): "Mississippi!"

TEACHER: "Well done, it's the Mississippi. Sara, can you tell me another name for the Mississippi?" (Teacher continues with the lesson.)

In the second vignette, it seems clear that the teacher recognized that the question–answer format was not likely to evoke a correct student response from Ming. She changed her expected method of response from vocal to demonstration, avoiding student embarrassment, allowing Ming to participate and receive public recognition, and ensuring that the question ended with a correct response.

Teachers, of course, can change the initial mode of presentation and the expected mode of response for a variety of common classroom situations. Tables 2 and 3 show examples.

TABLE 2
Ways To Change the Initial Mode of Presentation

Task	Initial Mode of Presentation	Modified Mode of Presentation
Copying board work	Vocal: Teacher tells students what to do (once) and goes from group to group with different directions.	Vocal: Tape-recorded directions allow students to hear the directions as many times as necessary to ensure comprehension.
Answering questions	Vocal: Teacher asks a single question and calls on a single student.	Written: Questions are preprinted and students practice correct responses within dyads. (Self-checking answer key is available to ensure accuracy.)

TABLE 3
Ways To Change the Mode of Response

Task	Initial Mode of Expected Response	Modified Mode of Expected Response
Answering questions	Vocal: Teacher asks a question and calls on a single student, anticipating a vocal response.	Written: Teacher asks a question, and students use "response cards," with all students participating.[1]
Completing math problems	Written: Teacher writes the page numbers and problem sets (e.g., odd numbers) for students to complete independently in a copybook.	Written: Problems are shown on the chalkboard and a teammate can help. Teacher provides the problem, and students complete interdependently with their partners.

[1] Response cards are cards or signs that students display in response to a teacher question. All students participate simultaneously (Heward, 1994).

Question 4

What does a teacher accomplish by modifying either the initial mode of presentation or the expected mode of response?

Individual Versus Group Consequences and Schedules of Reinforcement

Most students enjoy playing games, which generate excitement and motivation, and teachers typically do not have difficulty recruiting players. Games can be arranged to address instructional goals and can be played on an individual or group basis. On an individual level, students might be directed to "beat their best score" during whatever activity the game's goal is directed to achieve. On a group basis, members would cooperate during the game and share the same outcome. Individual and group games can be arranged to "pay off" on a continuous or intermittent schedule of reinforcement. When the contingency is continuous, all instances of the behavior are reinforced. When it is intermittent, only some responses produce the reinforcer. Table 4 shows the basic concept underlying each of these game arrangements.

TABLE 4
A Matrix of Game Strategies by Type of Reinforcement

	Individual	**Group**
Continuous	The individual student produces classwork responses, and each response produces a reinforcer (e.g., a student plays a computer-based game that is programmed to provide a vocal reinforcer for each correct response: "That's good!" "That's correct!" "Well done!").	The group (or subgroup) produces a response, and each response produces a reinforcer (e.g., during a teacher-directed game, choral responding in unison by the group produces a vocal praise statement by the teacher).
Intermittent	The individual student produces classwork responses, and only some of the responses produce a reinforcer (e.g., when the student completes a classwork assignment, he or she receives a coupon that is placed in a fishbowl; at the end of the day, he or she is eligible for a reinforcer during a drawing).	A group of students produce classwork responses, and only some of the responses produce a reinforcer. For instance, the teacher divides the class into teams, assignments are provided, and the team with the most assignments completed correctly within the time period is awarded the highest number of points. All teams are eligible for a base number of points, assuming a minimum level of achievement.

Question 5

> Provide examples of how to arrange an individual and group consequence using procedures associated with continuous and intermittent reinforcement.

_____

_____

_____

_____

_____

_____

_____

_____

Teaching

Seating Arrangement

Where students sit and how they are arranged in a classroom can make a difference in their academic productivity. Figure 2 shows four basic arrangements for classrooms: rows, clusters, horseshoe, and random. Depending on the tasks, some arrangements may be more conducive than others for completing an assignment. For instance, if the teacher is using a group-oriented, gamelike activity for the assignment, a clusters arrangement would probably be most appropriate. Students can exchange information across a table, view and hear vocal and nonvocal prompts more effectively, and work collaboratively. If an individual contingency is in effect, a rows arrangement may work best. In this case, the emphasis is on independent work and the rows arrangement would set the occasion for the student to work alone.

Helping Students Complete Classwork and Homework | 11

Rows

Clusters

Horseshoe

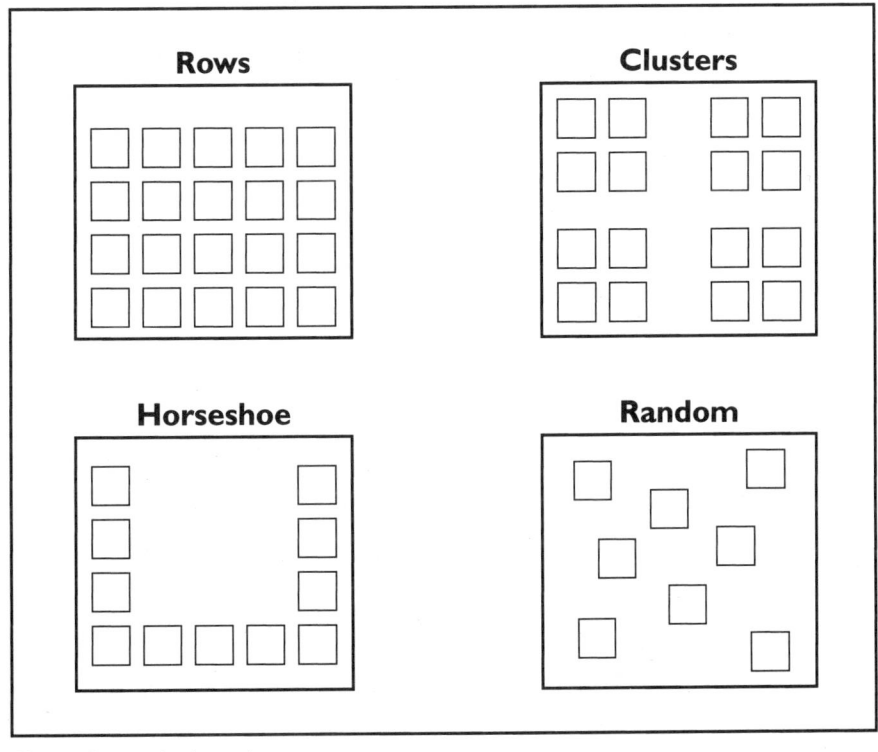

Random

Figure 2. Four basic seating arrangements.

Question 6

Under what conditions might a clusters arrangement be more conducive to learning than a rows arrangement? Give an example of when you might use a horseshoe arrangement.

_____
_____
_____
_____
_____

Correcting Student Errors

It is often said that the outcome of a useful instructional session depends in large measure on how the teacher corrects student errors. Essentially, teachers have two choices when it comes to correcting student errors during an instructional session. These alternatives are having the student, subsequent to the error, make either a passive or active response. The basic distinction between passive and active response modes can be stated as follows: In passive modes, students are not required to demonstrate the correct response in any form before the next instructional item is presented. In active modes of error correction, students make the correct response after hearing or seeing a model and before the next instructional task is presented. Active modes improve the quantity and quality of student responses. Data from research studies show that when students make active responses, their performance improves (Heward, 1994).

Question 7

> Describe the fundamental difference between an active and a passive response and explain why this difference is important.

_____

_____

_____

Charting Performance

Charting student performance can be an excellent way to motivate students. Students who see that their in-class work is improving are more likely to continue to work than students who do not receive visual feedback. Teachers can use cumulative and noncumulative graphs to portray student performance. The benefit of a cumulative graph is that student performance never decreases. Figure 3 shows an example of the use

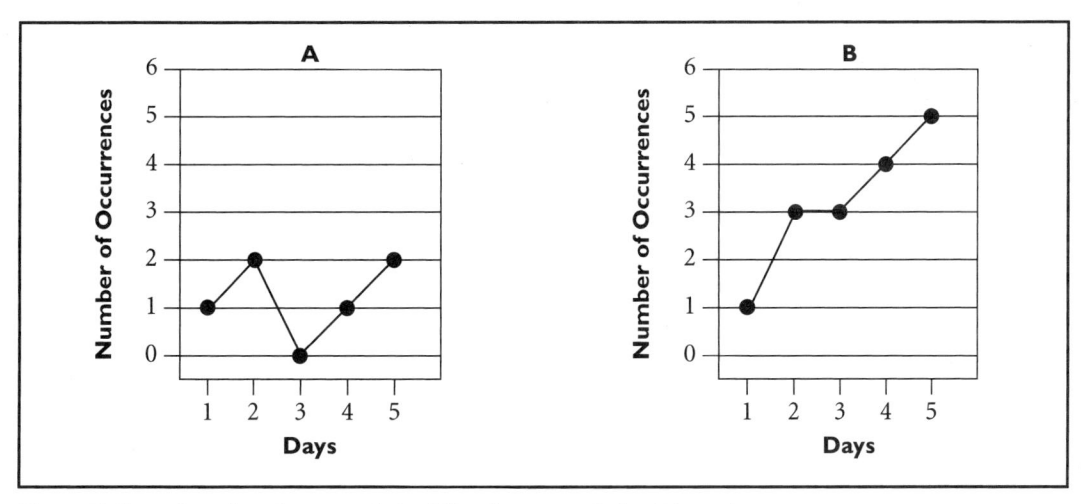

Figure 3. Same data plotted on cumulative (B) and noncumulative (A) graphs.

of cumulative and noncumulative graphs. Note that in the plot of scores on the left, when the student's performance was zero (session 3), the data show a decline in performance. The same data plotted on a cumulative graph (right) show a plateau for that day, meaning that the zero earned on Day 3 was added to the cumulative total from Day 2. Hence, the path reflects the same data (e.g., three correct). Student motivation to continue to work on in-class assignments can be enhanced when the record of their work shows an ascending trend. Depending on student ages, differences in ability, and the type of lesson, other types of graphs might also be considered for displaying in-class assignment completion.

Question 8

What is an advantage of plotting student in-class assignment completion data on a cumulative graph?

Postteaching

Grading Options

In-class productivity can be reinforced using a variety of grading options. The principal options include an Olympic scoring system (throw out the worst score), weighted grades (including grades for effort and product), and contractual grades. Table 5 shows a three-column matrix of such options, along with practical comments for implementation.

TABLE 5
Matrix of Grading Options

Type of Grading Option	Example	Practical Comments
Olympic Scoring System	The worst score in a series of scores earned over the semester is thrown out.	If a student starts slowly (i.e., performs poorly), knowing that his worst score is going to be tossed out may provide the incentive for the student to continue to try.
Weighted Grades	Suppose that a student has a multiple-part assignment (e.g., reading a book, taking notes, and writing a book report); different aspects of the report would be assigned relative weights.	The student could earn maximum points for those components of the report that are relative strengths, and lose minimum points for components that are not as strong.
Contractual Grades	Similar to weighted grades, except that the student recognizes when the assignment is presented just what the tasks and the associated reinforcers are. The student "strikes a deal" with the teacher to complete the assignment for an agreed-upon grade (the reinforcer).	Students enjoy contracts; they are flexible and they allow for active student responding.

Question 9

> Give an example from your own teaching situation of when you might use contractual grades.

_____

_____

_____

_____

PART II: Increasing Homework Productivity

Figure 4 shows a graphic that orients the teacher to four major components related to increasing homework productivity (Patton, 1994). These include management considerations, assignment considerations, the parents' roles, and the students' roles. The next section will address each of these components and provide practical tips for implementation.

Management Considerations

Management considerations describe the proactive steps a teacher can take to increase students' homework success. The next section addresses 10 steps teachers can employ.

☛ **Step 1: Assess homework skills.**

Imagine a third-grade math student, Rashad, who is unable to carry the remainder from the ones column to the tens column to perform basic

CONSIDERATIONS FOR HOMEWORK SUCCESS

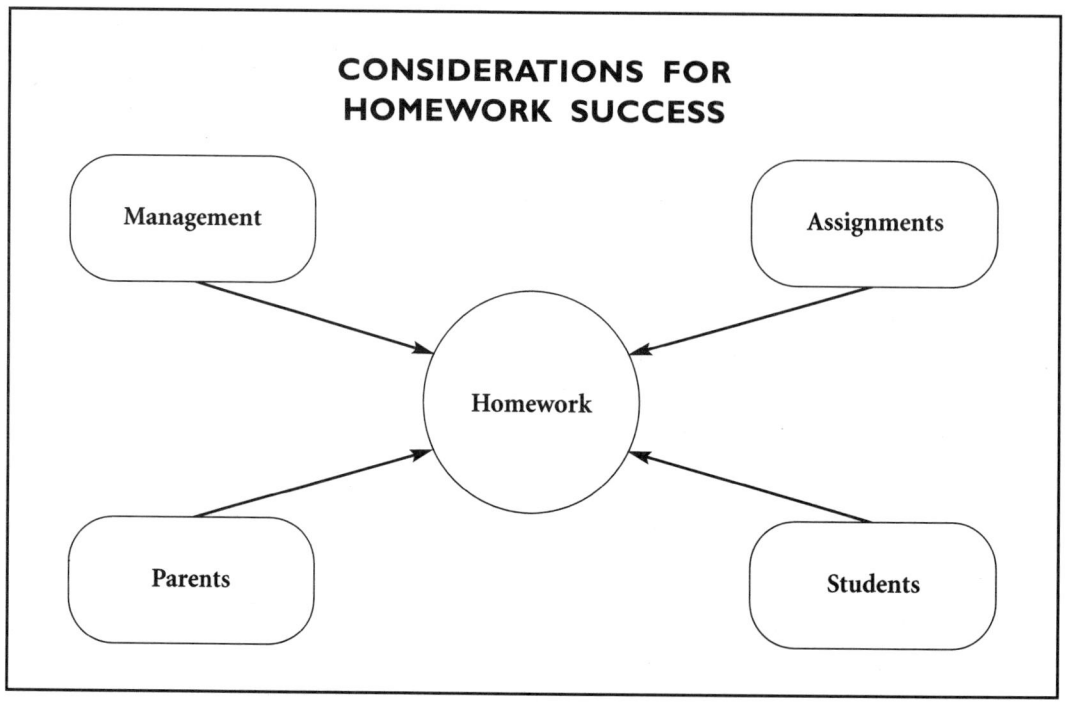

[Diagram: Management, Assignments, Parents, and Students all pointing to Homework at the center]

Figure 4. Major components related to increasing homework productivity. *Note.* Adapted from "Practical Recommendations for Using Homework with Students with Learning Disabilities," by J. R. Patton, 1994, *Journal of Learning Disabilities, 27*(9), pp. 570–578. Copyright 1994 by PRO-ED, Inc. Adapted with permission.

addition. Despite his earnest efforts, he cannot complete the addition problems assigned by his math teacher. Further, imagine a fourth-grade student, Corina, who struggles with the basics of printing. Unable to write legibly, she is unable to complete her writing composition assignment. What can teachers do to ensure that assignments are a good match with their students' current abilities? Before assigning homework, teachers should assess their students' current skills.

A task analysis is good way to assess homework skills. A task analysis is an ordered list of the steps, one leading to the next, that make up the behaviors a student must perform to complete an assignment.

Table 6 shows a short task analysis completed for a student for a math assignment involving the addition of two-digit numbers with regrouping.

TABLE 6
Short Task Analysis Completed for a Sample Student Involving the Addition of Two-Digit Numbers with Regrouping

Steps	Student Performance?
1. Adds the numbers in the ones column correctly and writes partial sum below the line	Yes
2. Carries the remainder to tens columns and writes it down	No
3. Adds the tens column, including the remainder, and writes down the partial sum	No

Question 10

What is a task analysis?

___

Using the task analysis, the teacher has recorded the student's performance on an addition assignment during an in-class observation. In the right column, the teacher has recorded *yes* or *no* to indicate the student's performance for each step of the assignment. Using this information, the teacher decides to do several in-class lessons on carrying the remainder to the tens column (Step 2). When the student demonstrates mastery of the skill in class, the teacher will assign homework on adding two-digit numbers with a remainder to provide additional practice.

Of course, a task analysis can be expanded or contracted depending on the student's needs. For instance, Table 7 shows two task analyses—one short and one long—that might be used to prepare frozen

TABLE 7
Short and Long Task Analyses for Preparing Frozen Pizza

Short Task Analysis	Long Task Analysis
1. Preheat oven to 400 degrees.	1. Preheat oven to 400 degrees.
2. Remove pizza from box.	2. Remove pizza box from refrigerator.
3. Place pizza on baking sheet.	3. Place pizza box on counter next to oven.
4. Place pizza in oven.	4. Open pizza box by pulling cardboard tab on side of box.
5. Set timer for 40 minutes.	5. Remove pizza from box and place on baking sheet.
6. When timer rings, remove pizza from oven.	6. Throw pizza box in garbage.
7. Place pizza on counter.	7. Open oven door.
8. Cut pizza into eight pie wedges.	8. Place baking sheet with pizza on top rack inside oven.
	9. Close oven door.
	10. Set timer for 40 minutes.
	11. When timer rings, place oven mitt on right (or left) hand.
	12. Open oven door.
	13. Remove baking sheet with pizza from oven with right (or left) hand and place on counter.
	14. Remove oven mitt.
	15. Remove knife from drawer.
	16. Cut pizza into eight pie wedges.
	17. Place knife in sink.

pizza at home as part of an adaptive daily living skills assignment for a high school student.

☞ **Step 2: Assign homework early.**

Establish homework as a part of the class routine early in the school year. An initial assignment should be given no later than the end of the first week of school, or sooner, if possible. Assigning homework early gives students more opportunities to practice skills at home and sends a message to parents that homework is critical to their child's academic development. Students may be less likely to complete homework if it is later added to an established routine.

☞ **Step 3: Establish a schedule for homework assignments.**

Many students, particularly those with special needs, learn best within a structured situation. Establishing a schedule for homework assignments teaches students that homework is a regular and important part of the class routine. You might, for example, assign science homework every Monday and Wednesday, and math homework every Tuesday and Friday. Whatever the specifics of your schedule, you should stick to it from week to week. Any changes in the schedule should be communicated clearly to the students in class.

At the junior and senior high school levels, consider other teachers' homework assignment schedules when designing yours. If you are giving an hour of assignments on Tuesday and Thursday, and two other teachers are giving comparable amounts of homework on these days, it may be difficult for students to keep pace. Coordinate your schedule with other teachers to ensure that students have a fair, balanced assignment schedule.

☞ **Step 4: Establish a routine for assigning, collecting, and evaluating homework.**

In addition to a regular homework schedule, establish a routine for assigning, collecting, and evaluating assignments. In the absence of a routine, it is easier for students (and you) to forget about homework. You should select a consistent time during the class period to issue your homework assignments. The end of the class period typically works best because students have already been exposed to the lesson material. However, ensure that enough time has been allotted to distribute, explain, and practice the assignment.

Consider providing a place (e.g., just inside the classroom door, on the windowsill, on the corner of your desk) and container (e.g., wire tray, basket, box) where students can submit their completed homework assignments upon entering the classroom the next day. The beginning of class is usually the best time to collect the previous day's assignment(s). Alternatively, you might assign a rotating helper to collect assignments. Students, especially at the elementary and middle school levels, who do well with or who are improving with homework might be homework helpers. Encourage students to ask questions about the assignment and incorporate answers to those questions into the day's lesson.

It is equally important to establish a routine for evaluating homework. Along with lesson planning, develop a regular schedule for grading homework. The sooner you grade and return assignments to students the better. Immediate feedback increases the likelihood that students will improve on future assignments and classwork.

Question 11

Assigning homework at the end of a class period is an acceptable strategy as long as what conditions are met?

_____
_____
_____
_____
_____

☞ **Step 5: Verify assignments (buddy system).**

Even when you deliver clear instructions, students may not always copy homework assignments accurately. A buddy system will help ensure that students have copied homework instructions correctly and completely. To implement the buddy system, pair students in your class and set aside a brief time for them to verify each other's assignments. Instruct one of the students to tell the teacher if there are discrepancies between the students' written directions. For junior and senior high school students with attention problems, it might be advisable for the buddy to meet his or her partner at the locker to ensure that all homework assignments are placed in the school bag before departing for the day (see Figure 5). Also, students can use this meeting opportunity to exchange phone numbers or e-mail addresses to contact each other if (a) an assignment is misunderstood, (b) a homework assignment needs to be discussed later in the evening, or (c) the student was absent previously and needs information to catch up with an assignment.

Figure 5. "Buddy check" at the locker before dismissal.

☛ **Step 6: Start in class.**

Once you have delivered homework directions, have students start the assignment in class. Having students start in class will show whether they understand your directions. Giving them a head start also reduces their perception that they have a lot of homework. Instruct students to complete the first one or two problems. As they work, check the accuracy of individual student answers, give positive and corrective feedback, and answer any questions.

☛ **Step 7: Use assignment books.**

Assignment books help students keep track of assignments and allow parents and teachers to communicate about students' progress. Every student should be given his or her own assignment book, and each page should contain a section for all academic subjects. Although the content of assignment books may vary, each subject section should contain spaces for students to write the following information: directions for the assignment, book chapter and page numbers (if applicable), point value of the assignment, and due date. Spaces for parents to write comments or to indicate that they have reviewed completed homework should be included. There should also be a section in the book for teacher comments and grades received on students' completed homework. Figure 6 shows an example of an assignment book for a fourth-grade student.

Subject	Assignment	Point Value	Due Date	Parent Initials	Parent Comments	Teacher Comments	Grade
Reading	Read pp. 10–15 in basal reader	5	12/20	TH	CH was able to complete this task w/in 20 minutes.	Questions were answered accurately	5/5
Math	Complete odd-numbered problems on p. 58	7	12/20	TH	CH was stuck on the last two problems.	Good effort with new material	6/7

Figure 6. Sample assignment book.

☛ **Step 8: Maintain regular communication with parents.**

The assignment book underscores the importance of maintaining regular communication with parents. Communicating with parents about homework at least once a week—either by telephone, in writing, by e-mail, or in person—maintains an open channel between teacher and parents. Regular communication allows you to assess students' progress at home anecdotally, answer any questions or concerns parents may have, and provide positive feedback for parents' efforts in helping their children with homework. Also, communication helps reduce potential inconsistencies between students' oral reports about their performance and their actual grades. Using postcards is still another way to communicate to parents on a regular basis (see Figure 7). A teacher would have a supply of preprinted postcards that would be mailed each week to parents to update them on their child's progress in assignment completion.

Date: _____ Teacher: _____

Subject: _____

Total Points (Cumulative) Earned/Possible So Far This Quarter: _____/_____

Present Grade (circle one): A A− B+ B B− C+ C C− D+ D D− F

Joshua's overall work this week has (improved, stayed the same, deteriorated) (circle one). Joshua is missing the following number of assignments: 0, 1, 2, 3, 4, more than 4, (circle one).

Figure 7. Sample of a preprinted postcard that a teacher could fill out and mail to parents each week. *Note.* From *The Educational Consultant: Helping Professionals, Parents, and Students in Inclusive Classrooms* (4th ed., p. 261), by T. Heron and K. Harris, 2001, Austin, TX: PRO-ED. Copyright 2001 by PRO-ED, Inc. Reprinted with permission.

Question 12

What benefits accrue from maintaining regular communication with parents?

Question 13

Describe how a postcard could be used to provide feedback to parents.

☛ **Step 9: Evaluate and provide feedback.**

Evaluate students' homework and provide feedback as soon as possible. Ideally, students should receive feedback about homework performance the day after they hand in a short-term assignment. This ensures that students receive relevant information on homework covering the current lesson or unit, and increases the likelihood of success on future assignments. Give positive and corrective feedback often on students' completion, accuracy, and legibility. Even if a student has made multiple errors on an assignment, be sure to provide positive feedback for that portion of the assignment that was done correctly. The proportion of positive (e.g., "Great summary of the story!") to corrective (e.g., "You forgot to use possessive.") comments should be three or four to one.

Feedback charts are also useful ways to provide individual students and the class with data about their individual and collective performances. Figure 8 shows a feedback chart based on the concept of "beat your best score" (Van Houten, 1984).

Name	Day 1	Day 2	Day 3	Day 4	Day 5	Week Total	Highest Day	Highest Previous Week
Christine	3	4	5	4	5	21	5	20
Kathy	4	2	4	3	5	18	5	17
Marge	2	2	2	5	5	16	5	15
Matt	1	1	3	4	3	12	4	12
Jennifer	5	5	5	5	5	25	5	24
Brooke	5	5	5	5	5	25	5	20
Jeff	1	0	3	4	3	11	4	12

Figure 8. Feedback chart. *Note.* Adapted from "Setting Up Performance Feedback Systems in the Classroom," by R. Van Houten, 1984. In W. L. Heward, T. E. Heron, D. S. Hill, and J. Trap-Porter (Eds.), *Focus on Behavior Analysis in Education* (p. 121), Columbus, OH: Merrill. Copyright 1984 by Bell & Howell. Adapted with permission.

Question 14

> Ideally, when should students receive feedback on their homework assignments?

_____

_____

_____

_____

☛ **Step 10: Establish contingencies for homework completion.**

Because students may often view homework as a burden, rewards and incentive systems provide useful ways to reinforce students' homework efforts and reduce or eliminate their negative perceptions. Table 8 shows examples of motivational strategies to increase homework completion.

TABLE 8
Motivational Strategies To Increase Homework Completion

1. Give a day off from homework for good performance.
2. Implement a lottery system in which completed assignments can be redeemed for a ticket in a classroom lottery.
3. Allow students who complete assignments to be classroom helpers for a day.
4. Provide points for completing assignments as part of already existing motivational systems.
5. Provide individual student recognition (e.g., student of the week, picture on the wall of the classroom, classroom announcement, special newsletter) for exceptional performance.
6. Provide stickers for completed assignments. A set number of stickers earns a reinforcer.

Question 15

Provide three examples of motivational strategies teachers can use to improve homework completion.

a. _____

_____

b. _____

_____

c. _____

_____

Assignment Considerations

There are a number of considerations that a teacher should keep in mind when designing and assigning homework. Nine principal considerations follow.

☞ **Step 1: Establish the relevance of the assignment.**

Students who do not complete homework often complain that it is unimportant. To be relevant, homework assignments should relate to what is taught in the classroom. Too often, teachers assign busywork in their classes. For example, students who might be reading a novel are given grammar worksheets to complete. Further, the teacher may never discuss the worksheets after they have been submitted. Teachers need to be clear in informing students about how homework contributes to their learning of particular content and to their grades because students will not be able to go the extra mile to make these connections.

Question 16

> List two ways a teacher can make assignments relevant to students.

a. _____

_____

_____

b. _____

_____

_____

☞ **Step 2: Select an appropriate homework activity.**

When selecting a homework assignment, be sure there is a purpose established ahead of time and that the assignment meets that purpose. Ideally, a homework assignment should align with the subject matter being covered in the classroom, providing an opportunity for further practice on the content discussed in class. For instance, when discussing measurement in an elementary math class, an appropriate homework activity might include measuring a number of specific items found in students' homes (e.g., width of refrigerator, length of bed, width of television, length of bathtub). In a middle school civics class, students might be asked to research the electoral process. When covering the stock market in a high school economics class, assign students to "invest" a certain amount of money in a stock of their choice and then check the newspaper or Internet daily to track their stock's progress.

Teachers should also ask themselves what target behaviors their assignments are intended to review, and if indeed those behaviors are required to complete the assigned task. These questions can be answered by asking two questions: (a) how are the students expected to respond to the assignment? and (b) why are the students responding as they are? When students answer problems on a worksheet, for example, are they really reading and considering the problems, or do all the problems require the same operation so that the students do not even have to read the problems to begin finding the answers? There are a number of additional questions teachers can ask themselves about an assignment that can help ensure an assigned task meets the intended purpose (see Table 9).

A teacher can learn a lot about how students solve problems by observing them work in class. How do the students tackle an assignment? Is it the way you intended? Are students practicing the target skill when completing the assignment? Consider the teacher who gives students a spelling assignment that requires them to underline misspelled words in a list only to have them take their spelling test that asks them to write words in isolation. Teachers can help their students succeed on those tests by at least requiring throughout the week the same tasks they expect on test day. For instance, students might work reciprocally in pairs, with one student dictating spelling words and the other student writing the correct spelling. In effect, the students would practice the target skill: written spelling.

In another example, note that Figure 9 shows a shaded box that blocks a narrative reading selection. As Vargas (1984) notes, a student could probably answer the question below the selection without having to read the passage.

TABLE 9
Teacher Self-Articulated Questions

1. Can students use pictures or other visual displays instead of words to answer questions on an assignment?

2. Do boldfaced words or the physical layout of the assignment give away answers, making it unnecessary for students to read the entire assignment?

3. Are students able to use common sense or clues from other questions to correctly answer questions about a reading passage without even reading it? (See Figure 9.)

4. On a worksheet, do all problems require the same operation to solve, allowing students to read only the first question before completing the entire page?

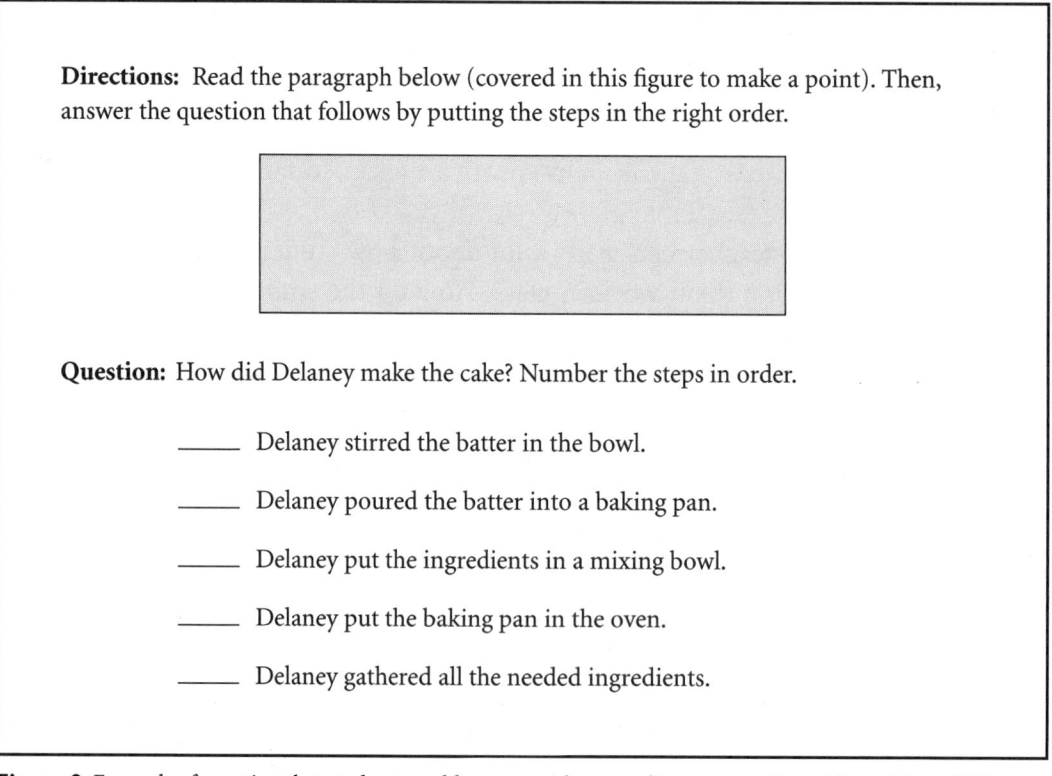

> **Directions:** Read the paragraph below (covered in this figure to make a point). Then, answer the question that follows by putting the steps in the right order.
>
> [shaded box]
>
> **Question:** How did Delaney make the cake? Number the steps in order.
>
> _____ Delaney stirred the batter in the bowl.
>
> _____ Delaney poured the batter into a baking pan.
>
> _____ Delaney put the ingredients in a mixing bowl.
>
> _____ Delaney put the baking pan in the oven.
>
> _____ Delaney gathered all the needed ingredients.

Figure 9. Example of question that students could answer without reading passage. *Note.* Adapted from "What Are Your Exercises Teaching?" by J. Vargas, 1984. In W. L. Heward, T. E. Heron, D. S. Hill, and J. Trap-Porter (Eds.), *Focus on Behavior Analysis in Education* (p. 134), Columbus, OH: Merrill. Copyright 1984 by Bell & Howell. Adapted with permission.

Question 17

> To ensure student success on a weekly quiz or test, a teacher might structure classwork or homework to achieve what objective?

_____

_____

_____

_____

☞ **Step 3: Ensure a high chance of success.**

It is important that homework tasks present students with frequent opportunities for success. Homework should provide students with practice on skills mastered, preparation for skills soon to be learned, or opportunities to enrich students' current knowledge on a given topic. Homework that is submitted with numerous errors was probably not appropriate. Students should have the skills to gain valuable practice from an assignment instead of being expected to teach themselves a new skill through the assignment.

There are several ways a teacher can help students with assignments in high reading requirement areas (e.g., social studies, science, psychology). Prior to assigning work out of the textbook, read the summary of the selection with the students. This can help put the lesson in context. Also, read all major headings and graphics within the chapter. Again, this helps focus the students' attention on the key points and ideas prior to reading the passage. You can go even further by examining the topic sentences of each paragraph and the boldface or key terms, and then reviewing the questions or exercises. Reviewing and discussing the content is beneficial for all students, giving them additional background and focusing their thinking. For students needing extra help (low-average students or students with special needs), you can highlight key words in study questions to help students locate answers; list the study questions in the order they appear in the reading passage; provide page numbers or paragraph numbers to help focus attention when seeking answers; preteach critical vocabulary; or highlight key words, phrases, or sentences in the text. Some teachers might believe this is more work on their part, but the payoff will be that more students understand and respond correctly to homework assignments, in turn creating richer classroom discussion about text content.

Question 18

Identify three ways that teachers can facilitate in-class assignment completion or homework completion when the reading demands of the tasks are high.

a. _____

b. _____

c. _____

☛ **Step 4: Select challenging but doable assignments.**

Although teachers want students to be successful with homework, teachers want them to be challenged as well. On the other hand, students who find homework too challenging will resist it. You must find the right balance between challenging and doable assignments. To do so, you often must be creative. Consider the following examples.

Ms. Riddle is teaching basic addition and subtraction to her first-grade students. She is trying to increase their fluency with the material by assigning numerous problems for homework. The students, however, are becoming bored with their addition and subtraction facts and are not completing their assignments. To make the assignments more interesting, Ms. Riddle embeds simple addition and subtraction facts in word problems she has made up about the students and teachers in her school. She finds that students have a renewed interest in the work because they enjoy reading the scenarios. Not only are the problems more interesting, but the students also have to work a little harder to figure out the answers.

Mr. Jenkins teaches social studies at a local high school. His students are studying a unit on military veterans. He assigns students to interview veterans and present their interviews to the class. This assignment is not particularly difficult because there is a high density of veterans in the area. Mr. Jenkins makes the assignment more challenging, however, when he requires students to videotape the interview and share it with their peers. This added twist makes each student go beyond a simple interview to design a quality presentation.

Question 19

> How can teachers generate assignments that are challenging and doable?

_____
_____
_____
_____

☛ **Step 5: Don't use homework as punishment.**

Students will dislike homework if it is given as punishment. Assigning repetitive sentences to write, for example, only makes homework aversive to students. Instead, keep students' attitudes about homework positive and help them view it as a learning opportunity rather than as punishment.

☛ **Step 6: Relate homework content to student interests.**

Students often find homework boring. Teachers can help students' attitudes about completing homework by incorporating various areas of interest into their assignments (see Table 10).

The more students can relate to their assignments and see how they apply to their learning and the real world, the more likely they are to maintain interest in completing the assignment.

☛ **Step 7: Vary assignments to avoid too much repetition.**

We have all experienced tasks that are so redundant we tend to doze off midway through them. Students are also unlikely to remain alert when directed to complete boring tasks. Hence, teachers should vary the

TABLE 10
Sample Assignments Tailored To Match Student Interests

Subject Area	Sample Assignments
Math	Rather than relying on generic word problems developed by textbook authors, incorporate students' names into various question scenarios; use real-life examples such as going to movies, concerts, or saving money for favorite items (e.g., video games, clothing, compact discs).
Language Arts/Writing	Instead of copying a business letter out of a book, have students write a business letter to a local business requesting company information or a company tour. Have students write a friendly letter to an actual friend or relative the student hasn't seen in a while.
Social Studies	Instead of memorizing cultural characteristics of an area, assign group presentations for which students must make or obtain pieces of a culture to share with the class. Have students contact someone in their area who is from a studied location or culture and videotape an interview with that person to share with the class.

content and types of assignments they give to all students. For older students, rather than sending home a worksheet or page out of a workbook, have them develop their own assignment to cover the content and then have them trade and complete each other's task. Instead of having elementary students underline the nouns and circle the verbs on a page out of their English book, let them complete the task using a page they are assigned to read for social studies or from a class novel. Variety in homework assignments will help maintain students' interest.

☛ **Step 8: Consider two dimensions of homework: completion and accuracy.**

It is not enough to have a classroom of students who do their homework completely, if their accuracy is low. An elementary student with attention deficit disorder may rush through his or her assignments to get them done, rather than taking the time to do them correctly. Such a pattern might even add to the student's confusion on certain topics. When the student does not take time to complete a task correctly, he might also practice incorrect responses. When this happens, students become more proficient at making errors.

To encourage and support students in completing homework accurately, consider these strategies:

- Be sure students understand the assignment. One of the best tests of comprehension is restatement. Providing time in class for students to begin the homework assignment allows them to try a few items before taking the task home. If students can verbalize or demonstrate what they are supposed to do, or if they are unsure of what the homework task requires, they can discuss the matter before going home.
- Grade homework regularly and return it promptly. When students see that you take the time to review their assignments and provide feedback, they are more apt to understand the importance of the task and to complete it correctly. It is also easier to convey the importance of an assignment and how it fits in to the bigger picture of learning when teachers review the work and provide feedback.
- Provide incentives for students to work accurately. Often, knowing an assignment will be graded is sufficient incentive for students to take their time to complete it to the best of their ability. For those who still seem to be rushing through assignments with no concern for their accuracy, try spot-checking assignments. Providing minirewards to the class or to individual students based on spot-checks for accuracy can motivate all students to have their assignments completed correctly. Teachers can easily complete spot-checks by selecting a couple of problems randomly and checking only those problems for accuracy. If the problems are answered correctly, the individual students or the whole class can be reinforced (e.g., extra 5 minutes at recess, early to lunch one day, 5 minutes of reading time at the end of the period, no homework passes).

☛ **Step 9: Consider the number of responses required versus the amount of time required to complete assignments.**

Although the amount of time students spend outside the classroom on school tasks is important in increasing their learning, you must also consider how students spend that time. Teachers should structure assignments to ensure high levels of active student response. For example, a common homework assignment for science or social studies involves reading a passage and answering questions about it. Typically, there are only 5 to 10 questions with a few key words to define. Instead of reading the selection and then answering the questions, students often go right to the questions and skim back through the reading to find the answers. Completing the assignment in this manner assures that much of the passage is left unread. Alternatively, teachers can develop worksheets to accompany the passage that embed questions throughout the reading. Consequently, students are likely to read more sections to respond to the questions as they work through the chapter.

Question 20

> How might a teacher avoid the predictable trap of assigning a social studies chapter to read with corresponding end-of-chapter questions, only to have students race to the end of the chapter and start responding without first having read the entire chapter?

Parents' Roles

Families have an important role in homework success. Parents can do a lot to encourage and support the homework habits of their children. Whether the child is in elementary, middle, or high school, there are systems parents can establish in the home to reinforce appropriate homework habits. Teachers can help parents establish these systems by educating them on the importance of doing so and by offering suggestions and support as they get started. The following are some examples of what parents can do.

☞ **Step 1: Create a supportive environment.**

Parents can support their children on a basic level when they provide an environment in which their children can work. There are six key areas to consider.

1. *Find a place away from distractions where noise can be kept to a minimum.* Many students try to convince their parents that they are able to work best in their bedroom with the stereo blaring or with the television on, but few students are able to get optimum benefits from a work environment that is so distracting (see Figure 10). A quiet place where the student can focus on his or her work is most conducive to productivity.

Figure 10. Distracting homework environment.

2. *Establish one location for homework completion.* When looking for this location, there are a few points to keep in mind. For elementary children, try to avoid the bedroom. There are usually too many distractions in a child's bedroom that diminish study time. Further, it is hard to monitor a child's habits when he or she is out of sight. Use the bedroom as an option only when it is clear the child has good independent study habits. Also, find a place that is well-lighted and furnished with a flat writing surface and a chair. Parents should avoid having children use couches or easy chairs as they may set the occasion for daydreaming and catnapping.

3. *Provide the materials the child will need to complete the assignment before he or she begins.* Many students sit down to work on an assignment only to have to get up after a couple of minutes to sharpen a pencil, find an eraser, get more paper, find a dictionary, and so forth. Parents can help reduce the number of "excuses" to leave a work area when necessary materials are kept near the child's work area. Items parents might consider having on hand include pencils, pens, and other supplies. These items can be kept in a midsized box, tub, or basket.

4. *Control and limit others' access to the study area during homework time.* Children are easily distracted. Allowing a child to work in a center of activity in the household can lead to frequent interruptions. Frequent interruptions can produce lapses in concentration and make it difficult to maintain continuity of effort toward a task. It is common for children to want to complete their homework at the kitchen table. However, this is usually the area in a house that gets the most action—siblings coming in and out, the dog running through the room, mom or dad making dinner, or the phone ringing. If the kitchen table must be used, consider posting a sign that requests quiet (see Figure 11).

5. *Schedule a set time each day for homework completion.* As much as possible, parents should make completing homework a routine in the home. Whether it be as soon as children get home or after they have had dinner and rested a bit, finding a set work time each day helps reinforce to children the value of homework and its status as a normal part of the daily routine. On the other hand, parents who work hard to ensure their children make it to soccer practice, gymnastics, and piano lessons, yet allow their children to complete homework as part of the

```
┌─────────────────────────────────────┐
│                                     │
│      ┌───────────────────────┐      │
│      │                       │      │
│      │    Quiet Please:      │      │
│      │                       │      │
│      │   Genius at Work !!   │      │
│      │                       │      │
│      └───────────────────────┘      │
│                                     │
└─────────────────────────────────────┘
```

Figure 11. Quiet sign.

last-minute morning rush before heading out the door the next morning, are sending a very different message about the importance of homework.

6. *Be good work models in the home.* These days, many adults no longer leave work at the office. One commonly hears of mothers working on graduate degrees and fathers bringing home their laptops to meet time-sensitive deadlines. Parents participating in such activities can provide wonderful work models for their children. Working in a quiet place alongside their children can create an atmosphere of mutual support and respect.

☞ **Step 2: Encourage and reinforce effort.**

Many parents believe that showing an interest in schoolwork should come naturally to students. When their children do not show an interest, attempts to motivate them are often punitive. Although punitive measures may be effective on a short-term basis, they usually are ineffective in the long run. Forcing children to complete their homework with the threat of some negative consequence puts a parent in the role of punisher and fosters a negative relationship. Motivation should instead be positive, so that children will be more likely to complete homework in the future.

Parents have at their disposal a variety of reinforcers they can use to motivate their children to complete homework. Often, by spending a little time observing their child, parents can identify potential motivators that cost little or no money and are desired by their child (e.g., earning a later bedtime, sleepover privileges, having a friend over for dinner, extra television time, practice driving time). Educate parents on the following guidelines for using reinforcement: (a) start with an incremental reward for a small task that can be earned easily (so student will quickly "buy into the game"), (b) have the child select his or her own reward when possible (e.g., choose the family video), (c) vary the rewards, (d) do not make the reward something the child can't live without (e.g., dinner), and (e) do not start out with a delayed reward the student requires days or even weeks to obtain.

☞ **Step 3: Maintain involvement.**

Parents can maintain involvement with their child's homework in a few ways. First, they should maintain regular communication with the classroom teacher. In this way, parents can stay informed of what homework assignments have been issued and when they are due. Parents can help ensure they get the assignment book each evening by establishing set consequences for when the books do and do not make it home. That is, students can only watch television, play outside, get out their video games, or go to the mall when their homework is finished. A prescribed homework time takes away the incentive for students to rush through their work, completing it illegibly or incorrectly just so they can get it done and do something more fun.

Second, parents should be available when their children are working on assignments. This does not necessarily mean sitting right next to the child throughout his or her completion of the assignment. Being in the house and available to help if questions arise is usually all that is needed. Parents can also take a more active role by helping their child break tasks into workable parts, helping them prioritize assignment order, and providing a model for a difficult series of problems.

Third, for those assignments in which parents are unable to help (e.g., higher level math assignment that parents have forgotten how to complete, written responses to passages parents have not read or to lectures they have not heard), parents can still evaluate, at least on a cosmetic level, the final product. Parents can review their child's homework to ensure he or she followed the directions and to check for proper headings, logical organization of the content, legibility of the paper, and proper sentence structure and mechanics. Providing even this minimal level of support can show the child that homework is important. Parents who lack the literacy skills to do these tasks can be encouraged to enlist the cooperation of another family member or friend to help.

☛ Step 4: Communicate with teachers.

Communication between the home and school is critical for homework success. Children need to know that their parents are a part of their education and not only support it, but will actively contribute to it via direct communication with teachers. There are a number of ways parents and teachers can communicate. One of the most common ways involves using an assignment book or daily planner. Many schools are supplying these for all students, with the intended goal of providing an easy means of communicating with families. Parents can maintain regular communication with their child's teacher(s) by writing notes or comments in the child's planner. Comments might include how long it took the child to complete the assignment, what areas he or she found particularly easy or difficult, and notes about the effort the child put forth. In addition to the information provided in the notes, teachers learn that parents are involved and support their efforts at home. Teachers working with parents should encourage them to be consistent in their expectation to see their child's assignment log every day. If, despite best efforts to be positive, students fail to take their assignment books home and/or their work seriously, parents should be encouraged to provide the appropriate restrictive consequences.

☛ Step 5: Seek additional training.

Some parents do not feel comfortable assisting their children with homework. Either they believe that it is the school's job to teach and homework should not require adult assistance, or they find themselves helping too much, sometimes even to the point of completing the assignment for their child. Parents who can identify their weaknesses with respect to providing support can help themselves and their children by seeking additional training. Parents can obtain training through area resource centers, district-sponsored workshops, or community-based parent groups.

Question 21

> Suggest three ways that parents might increase their involvement and communication with the teacher with respect to assigned classwork and homework for their child.

a. _____

_____

b. _____

_____

c. _____

_____

Students' Roles

As a teacher, you can promote your students' roles in homework success. The following are three critical support skills and suggestions for how to accomplish this goal.

☛ **Step 1: Use recruiting skills.**

Despite your best efforts, you are unlikely to anticipate every query that students may have about their assignments. Unless you have a small class or extra staff, it may also be difficult to deliver positive and corrective feedback to students in a timely way. To become successful independent learners, students may need to demonstrate a range of recruiting, questioning, and feedback skills with the teacher, without needing additional teacher prompts to do so. Because many students are unlikely to demonstrate appropriate recruiting skills on their own, it may be necessary to teach them recruiting directly, using model, lead, and test strategies within a role-playing scenario (Alber, Heward, & Hippler, 1999).

Question 22

> Why might it be necessary to teach student recruitment skills directly?

▶ **Step 2: Use self-management skills.**

Students must demonstrate self-management skills to complete homework successfully. Students who are poor self-managers are often disorganized and fail to complete homework accurately or on time. Self-management skills include the ability to copy assignments correctly, gather and bring home the necessary materials, set aside time to complete homework, ask parents questions when necessary, solicit parents to check homework for accuracy, complete homework on time, return homework to school, and submit homework to the teacher. Although self-management is beyond the scope of this booklet, you should explain the importance of these skills to your students and encourage parents to reinforce the importance of self-management with their children.

Question 23

How is self-management defined as it relates to homework completion?

_____

_____

_____

_____

_____

☞ Step 3: Assume responsibility for homework.

Students must assume responsibility for homework. If students do not understand the importance of homework, they are unlikely to complete it. Unfortunately, most students are unlikely to develop responsibility for homework on their own. You should explain to your students the importance of homework to the learning process, reinforce homework completion, and encourage parents to stress the importance of homework.

Teachers and parents can promote responsibility for homework in the following ways. At the elementary and middle school levels, post outstanding or improved assignments in a highly visible place (e.g., on a bulletin board, classroom wall, or refrigerator). At the high school level, acknowledge outstanding or improved homework performance in progress reports and notes to parents and other teachers. At all grade levels, give students specific, positive feedback on what you liked about their homework (e.g., answered all questions correctly, expressed creative ideas, solved a difficult problem). Individually and collectively, these strategies will help students assume more responsibility for their work.

Question 24

Discuss ways that students can be directed to assume more responsibility for their homework.

FINAL EXAMINATION

1. How does the matrix shown in Table 1 assist teachers with programming in-class assignments?

2. What is an effect of having students arranged in tutor–tutee dyads with respect to practice and reinforcement?

3. Define cooperative learning and state main and collateral effects that can be achieved by implementing it.

4. What does a teacher accomplish by modifying either the initial mode of presentation or the expected mode of response?

5. Provide examples of how to arrange an individual and group consequence using procedures associated with continuous and intermittent reinforcement.

6. Under what conditions might a clusters seating arrangement be more conducive to learning than a rows seating arrangement? Give an example of when you might use a horseshoe seating arrangement.

7. Describe the fundamental difference between an active and a passive response and explain why this difference is important.

8. What is an advantage of plotting student in-class assignment completion data on a cumulative graph?

9. Give an example from your own teaching situation of when you might use contractual grades.

10. What is a task analysis?

11. Assigning homework at the end of a class period is an acceptable strategy as long as what conditions are met?

12. What benefits accrue from maintaining regular communication with parents?

13. Describe how a postcard could be used to provide feedback to parents.

14. Ideally, when should students receive feedback on their homework assignments?

15. Provide three examples of motivational strategies teachers can use to improve homework completion.

   a. _____

   b. _____

   c. _____

16. List two ways a teacher can make assignments relevant to students.

   a. _____
   _____

   b. _____
   _____

17. To ensure student success on a weekly quiz or test, a teacher might structure classwork or homework to achieve what objective?

   _____
   _____
   _____
   _____

18. Identify three ways that teachers can facilitate in-class assignment completion or homework completion when the reading demands of the tasks are high.

   a. _____

   b. _____

   c. _____

19. How can teachers generate assignments that are challenging and doable?

   _____
   _____
   _____
   _____

20. How might a teacher avoid the predictable trap of assigning a social studies chapter to read with corresponding end-of-chapter questions, only to have students race to the end of the chapter and start responding without first having read the entire chapter?

21. Suggest three ways that parents might increase their involvement and communication with the teacher with respect to assigned classwork and homework for their child.

    a.

    b.

    c.

22. Why might it be necessary to teach student recruitment skills directly?

23. How is self-management defined as it relates to homework completion?

24. Discuss ways that students can be directed to assume more responsibility for their homework.

ANSWER KEY

1. This matrix is helpful because it allows the teacher to arrange specific contingencies to increase class productivity based on the principal sequences by which teaching occurs, and within the various contextual arrangements that exist in the classroom.

2. Having tutor–tutee dyads increases the number of active response opportunities (practice), positive and corrective feedback events, and reinforcement statements for correct responses. Dyads can generate many more practice opportunities and feedback and reinforcement events than teachers can provide themselves.

3. Cooperative learning is defined as small groups of students working in teams to complete a task or common objective. These arrangements serve as viable alternatives for meeting the individual needs of students, especially those students who might have special needs. A main effect is that students experience interdependence during face-to-face interactions with peers, and the efforts of all members are needed for group accomplishment of the goal (i.e., productivity with the task). As important collateral effects, student leadership, decision-making ability, trust building, and conflict-management skills can be learned.

4. When teachers vary the initial mode of presentation and/or the expected mode of response, they set the occasion for students to provide correct responses in the classroom, thereby increasing active student responses, maintaining motivation, and reducing the negative effects of not being able to respond to the original question.

5. Answers will vary.

6. Anytime that a teacher uses a group-oriented, gamelike activity for the assignment, a clusters arrangement would be a more appropriate configuration for the class. In clusters, students can exchange information across a table, view and hear vocal and nonvocal prompts more effectively, and work collaboratively. Example answers will vary.

7. The basic distinction between passive and active response modes is the following: In passive modes, students are not required to demonstrate the correct response in any form before the next instructional item is presented. In active modes, students are required to make a correct response before the next instructional task is presented. Active responses are better because they tend to improve the quantity and quality of student responses.

8. The benefit of a cumulative graph is that student performance is never shown to decrease: It either ascends or plateaus.

9. Answers will vary.

10. A task analysis is an ordered list of the steps, one leading to the next, that make up the behaviors a student must perform to complete an assignment.

11. Assigning homework at the end of class is acceptable as long as enough time has been allotted to distribute, explain, and practice the assignment.

12. Regular communication with parents allows the teacher to assess students' homework progress at home, answer any questions or concerns parents may have, and provide positive feedback to parents for helping with homework. It may also reduce inconsistencies between students' reports of progress to parents and their actual grades.

13. Postcards that inform parents of student assignment completion performance can be mailed on a weekly basis. Parents can then be aware of their child's performance status relative to these assignments.

14. Students should receive feedback about their homework the day after they hand in an assignment.

15. Three motivational strategies teachers can use to improve homework completion are (a) providing a "day off" for good homework performance, (b) allowing students who complete assignments to be classroom helpers for the day, and (c) providing individual student recognition (e.g., student of the week, student picture on the wall of the classroom, classroom announcement, special newsletter) for exceptional performance.

16. A teacher can make assignments relevant to students by (a) avoiding busywork and repetitive assignments, (b) discussing worksheets and other assignments with students after they have been submitted, and (c) explaining to students how homework relates to students' grades and the lesson content.

17. Teachers might structure classwork or homework to solicit the same responses expected on a weekly quiz or test.

18. Teachers might (a) read the summary of the selection with the students; (b) read all major headings and graphics within the chapter with students; (c) examine the topic sentences of each paragraph; (d) examine the boldface terms; (e) review the questions or exercises that are assigned; (f) highlight key words in study questions; (g) list the study questions in the order they appear in the reading passage; (h) provide page numbers or paragraph numbers to help focus students' attention when seeking answers; (i) preteach critical vocabulary; or (j) highlight key words, phrases, or sentences in the text.

19. Teachers can generate assignments that are challenging, but doable, by assessing and understanding the ability levels of their students and being creative in the development of assignments.

20. Teachers might develop worksheets that accompany the reading and have questions on various points throughout the passage embedded in them. Students would then have to read through the entire selection to correctly complete the worksheets.

21. Parents might increase their involvement and communication with teachers with respect to assigned classwork and homework by (a) creating a supportive environment; (b) encouraging and reinforcing student effort; (c) maintaining involvement; (d) communicating with teachers through an assignment book; and/or (e) seeking additional training.

22. Student recruitment skills are important because they allow students to gain extra help when it is needed, obtain feedback on their work, get more work done, earn higher scores, and feel good about their skills. They may need to be taught directly because students do not usually learn to perform these skills on their own.

23. As it relates to homework, self-management skills include the ability to copy assignments correctly, gather and bring home the necessary materials, set aside time to complete homework, ask parents questions when necessary, solicit parents to check homework for accuracy, complete homework on time, return homework to school, and submit homework to the teacher.

24. Answers will vary.

REFERENCES AND FURTHER READINGS

Alber, S., Heward, W. L., & Hippler, B. (1999). Teaching middle school students with learning disabilities to recruit positive teacher attention. *Exceptional Children, 62,* 253–270.

Black, S. (1997). The truth about homework: What the research says might surprise you. *The American School Board Journal,* 48–51.

Bryan, T., & Sullivan-Burstein, K., (1997). Homework how-to's. *Teaching Exceptional Children, 29*(6), 32–37.

Callahan, K., Rademacher, J. A., & Hildreth, B. L. (1998). The effect of parent participation in strategies to improve the homework performance of students who are at risk. *Remedial and Special Education, 19*(3), 131–141.

Cooper, H., & Nye, B. (1994). Homework for students with learning disabilities: The implications for policy and practice. *Journal of Learning Disabilities, 27*(8), 470–479.

Epstein, M. H., Polloway, E. A., Foley, R. M., & Patton, J. R. (1993). Homework: A comparison of teachers' and parents' perceptions of the problems experienced by students identified as having behavioral disorders, learning disabilities, or no disabilities. *Remedial and Special Education, 14*(5), 40–50.

Greenwood, C. R., Delquadri, J. C., & Hall, R. V. (1984). Opportunity to respond and student achievement performance. In W. L. Heward, T. E. Heron, D. S. Hill, & J. Trap-Porter (Eds.), *Focus on behavior analysis in education* (pp. 58–88). Columbus, OH: Merrill.

Heron, T. E., & Harris, K. C. (2001). *The educational consultant: Helping professionals, parents, and students in inclusive classrooms* (4th ed.). Austin, TX: PRO-ED.

Heward, W. L. (1994). Three "low tech" strategies for increasing the frequency of active student response during group instruction. In R. Gardner, III, D. M. Sainato, J. O. Cooper, T. E. Heron, W. L. Heward, J. Eshleman, et al. (Eds.), *Behavior analysis in education: Focus on measurably superior instruction* (pp. 283–320). Pacific Grove, CA: Brooks/Cole.

Jayanthi, M., Bursuck, W., Epstein, M. H., & Polloway, E. A. (1997). Strategies for successful homework. *Teaching Exceptional Children, 30*(1), 4–7.

Jayanthi, M., Nelson, J. S., Sawyer, V., Bursuck, W. D., & Epstein, M. H. (1995). Homework-communication problems among parents, classroom teachers, and special education teachers: An exploratory study. *Remedial and Special Education, 16*(2), 102–116.

Jenson, W. R., Sheridan, S. M., Olympia, D., & Andrews, D. (1994). Homework and students with learning disabilities and behavior disorders: A practical, parent-based approach. *Journal of Learning Disabilities, 27*(9), 538–548.

Kay, P. J., Fitzgerald, M., Paradee, C., & Mellencamp, A. (1994). Making homework work at home: The parent's perspective. *Journal of Learning Disabilities, 27*(9), 550–561.

Patton, J. R. (1994). Practical recommendations for using homework with students with learning disabilities. *Journal of Learning Disabilities, 27*(9), 570–578.

Peters, M., & Heron, T. E. (1993). When the best is not good enough: An examination of best practice. *Journal of Special Education, 26*(4), 371–385.

Van Houten, R. (1984). Setting up performance feedback systems in the classroom. In W. L. Heward, T. E. Heron, D. S. Hill, & J. Trap-Porter (Eds.), *Focus on behavior analysis in education* (pp. 114–125). Columbus, OH: Merrill.

Vargas, J. S. (1984). What are your exercises teaching? An analysis of stimulus control in instructional materials. In W. L. Heward, T. E. Heron, D. S. Hill, & J. Trap-Porter (Eds.), *Focus on behavior analysis in education* (pp. 126–141). Columbus, OH: Merrill.

Wood, J. W. (2002). *Adapting instruction to accommodate students in inclusive settings* (4th ed.). Upper Saddle River, NJ: Merrill Prentice Hall.

ABOUT THE AUTHORS

Timothy E. Heron received his BA, MEd, and EdD from Temple University. He is a professor in the School of Physical Activity and Educational Services at The Ohio State University. Dr. Heron also served as an educational consultant to Children's Hospital Learning Disability Clinic in Columbus, Ohio. Prior to his appointment, Dr. Heron served as a developmental and day-care supervisor for students with brain injury and cerebral palsy, taught students with learning disabilities, and supervised a training program for resource room teachers in an inner-city school. He has published several books and articles, presented numerous papers at regional, national, and international conferences, and has served as a consultant to teachers, parents, and administrators on issues related to applied behavior analysis, tutoring systems, inclusion, and teacher and parent training.

Brooke J. Hippler received her BS, MA, and PhD from The Ohio State University. She is a special education coordinator for the Groveport Madison Local School District in Groveport, Ohio. Dr. Hippler also teaches undergraduate and graduate level classes at The Ohio State University, provides workshops to parents and teachers on the effective use of homework, and is responsible for training school district staff in nonviolent crisis prevention. Prior to obtaining her current position, Dr. Hippler was a special education teacher. She has presented papers at local, state, and national conferences, and has conducted research in the areas of homework, self-management, and instructional strategies for beginning teachers.

Matthew J. Tincani received his BA degree from West Chester University of Pennsylvania, his MEd from Temple University, and his PhD from The Ohio State University. Currently, he is a faculty member at the University of Nevada Las Vegas. Dr. Tincani was a teacher and consultant to children and adults with moderate and severe disabilities. He has presented papers at regional, national, and international conferences, consulted with teachers on a variety of classroom management and instructional issues, and conducted research in the area of effective instruction.

Use the new, fast-and-free, "orders only" fax number. 1-800-FXPROED
PRO-ED, 8700 Shoal Creek Boulevard, Austin, Texas 78757-6897   1-800/897-3202

Credit Card/PO Billing Address

Name _____

Address _____

_____

_____

Ship To: Telephone Number _____

Name _____

Address _____

_____

_____

GUARANTEE

All products are sold on 30-day approval. If you are not satisfied, you can return any product within 30 days. Please contact our office to receive authorization and necessary shipping instructions for returns. Prepaid orders will receive prompt refund, less handling charges. **Please use our fax number (1-800-FXPROED or 1-800/397-7633)!**

PAYMENT: All orders must be prepaid in full in U.S. funds by check or money order payable to PRO-ED, Inc., or by credit card. Open accounts are available to bookstores, public schools, libraries, institutions, and corporations. Please prepay first order and send full credit information to open an account.

Billing Authorization (must be completed or we cannot bill)

Purchase Order Number _____

❑ **Payment Enclosed**

Credit Card ❑ VISA ❑ MasterCard ❑ AMEX ❑ Discover

NOTE: Credit card billing address at top left must be completed if your order is charged to a credit card.

Authorized Signature _____

Card Number _____

Expiration Date _____

If prices on your order are incorrect, we reserve the right to exceed the amount up to 10% unless otherwise stated on your order. Terms are net, F.O.B. Austin, Texas; prices are subject to change without notice. ALL ORDERS MUST BE PAID IN U.S. FUNDS.

Quantity	Prod. No.	Book Title	Unit Price	Total
	10467	*How To Help Students Remain Seated*	$ 9.00	
	10468	*How To Deal Effectively with Lying, Stealing, and Cheating*	$ 9.00	
	10469	*How To Prevent and Safely Manage Physical Aggression and Property Destruction*	$ 9.00	
	10470	*How To Help Students Complete Classwork and Homework Assignments*	$ 9.00	
	10471	*How To Help Students Play and Work Together*	$ 9.00	
	10472	*How To Deal with Students Who Challenge and Defy Authority*	$ 9.00	
	10473	*How To Deal Effectively with Whining and Tantrum Behaviors*	$ 9.00	
	10474	*How To Help Students Follow Directions, Pay Attention, and Stay on Task*	$ 9.00	
	10465	All 8 *How To* titles	$56.00	

Product Total _____

Handling, Postage, and Carrying Charges
(U.S. add 10%; Canada add 15%; others add 20%. Minimum charge $1.00) _____

Subtotal _____

Texas residents ONLY add 8.25% sales tax or WRITE IN TAX-EXEMPT NUMBER _____

Grand Total (U.S. Funds Only) _____

PRO-ED, Inc.   8700 Shoal Creek Boulevard   Austin, Texas 78757-6897   Online store www.proedinc.com (secure server)

NOTES

NOTES